FRIENDSHIP
Growing Side by Side

*12 Studies
for individuals or groups*

Carolyn Nystrom

With Notes for Leaders

InterVarsity Press
Downers Grove, Illinois

21	20	19	18	17	16	15	14	13	12	11	10	9	8	7	6	5	4	3	2	1
14	13	12	11	10	09	08	07	06	05	04	03	02	01	00	99	98	97	96		

Contents

Getting the Most
from LifeGuide® Bible Studies

Many of us long to fill our minds and our lives with Scripture. We desire to be transformed by its message. LifeGuide® Bible Studies are designed to be an exciting and challenging way to do just that. They help us to be guided by God's Word in every area of life.

How They Work

LifeGuides have a number of distinctive features. Perhaps the most important is that they are *inductive* rather than *deductive*. In other words, they lead us to *discover* what the Bible says rather than simply *telling* us what it says.

They are also thought-provoking. They help us to think about the meaning of the passage so that we can truly understand what the author is saying. The questions require more than one-word answers.

The studies are personal. Questions expose us to the promises, assurances, exhortations and challenges of God's Word. They are designed to allow the Scriptures to renew our minds so that we can be transformed by the Spirit of God. This is the ultimate goal of all Bible study.

The studies are versatile. They are designed for student, neighborhood and church groups. They are also effective for individual study.

How They're Put Together

LifeGuides also have a distinctive format. Each study need take no more than forty-five minutes in a group setting or thirty minutes in personal study—unless you choose to take more time.

The studies can be used within a quarter system in a church and fit well in a semester or trimester system on a college campus. If a guide has more than thirteen studies, it is divided into two or occasionally three parts of approximately twelve studies each.

LifeGuides use a workbook format. Space is provided for writing answers to each question. This is ideal for personal study and allows group members to prepare in advance for the discussion.

The studies also contain leader's notes. They show how to lead a group discussion, provide additional background information on certain questions, give helpful tips on group dynamics and suggest ways to deal with problems which may arise during the discussion. With such helps, someone with little or no experience can lead an effective study.

Suggestions for Individual Study

1. As you begin each study, pray that God will help you to understand and apply the passage to your life.

2. Read and reread the assigned Bible passage to familiarize yourself with what the author is saying. In the case of book studies, you may want to read through the entire book prior to the first study. This will give you a helpful overview of its contents.

3. A good modern translation of the Bible, rather than the King James Version or a paraphrase, will give you the most help. The New International Version, the New American Standard Bible and the Revised Standard Version are all recommended. However, the questions in this guide are based on the New International Version.

4. Write your answers in the space provided in the study guide. This will help you to express your understanding of the passage clearly.

5. It might be good to have a Bible dictionary handy. Use it to look up any unfamiliar words, names or places.

Suggestions for Group Study

1. Come to the study prepared. Follow the suggestions for individual study mentioned above. You will find that careful preparation will greatly enrich your time spent in group discussion.

2. Be willing to participate in the discussion. The leader of your group will not be lecturing. Instead, he or she will be encouraging the members of the group to discuss what they have learned from the passage. The leader will be asking the questions that are found in this guide. Plan to share what God has taught you in your individual study.

3. Stick to the passage being studied. Your answers should be based on the verses which are the focus of the discussion and not on outside authorities such as commentaries or speakers. This guide deliberately avoids jumping from book to book or passage to passage. Each study focuses on only one

passage. Book studies are generally designed to lead you through the book in the order in which it was written. This will help you follow the author's argument.

4. Be sensitive to the other members of the group. Listen attentively when they share what they have learned. You may be surprised by their insights! Link what you say to the comments of others so the group stays on the topic. Also, be affirming whenever you can. This will encourage some of the more hesitant members of the group to participate.

5. Be careful not to dominate the discussion. We are sometimes so eager to share what we have learned that we leave too little opportunity for others to respond. By all means participate! But allow others to also.

6. Expect God to teach you through the passage being discussed and through the other members of the group. Pray that you will have an enjoyable and profitable time together.

7. If you are the discussion leader, you will find additional suggestions and helpful ideas for each study in the leader's notes. These are found at the back of the guide.

Introducing Friendship

I didn't have many friends when I was growing up. There were lots of reasons: I lived in a rural community without transportation; there were economic differences between our family and those around us (I was poor); my church emphasized separation; my family masked its fear of outsiders by intentionally closing itself off; my bookish nature—in a culture that valued action and practicality. (Students with A's were not welcomed in my high school—except by a few teachers who weren't welcomed either.) But lest I attach all blame for my friendlessness to outside influences, I now know that my own arrogance was insufferable to those few who might have been willing to climb the barriers toward friendship.

There were advantages to this early deprivation of friendship. I learned to enjoy solitude. I learned to find personal projects that bring me satisfaction. (I've never been bored for more than an hour or two in my life.) I learned independence. It mystified me in college that other students ran around trying to find someone to go meals with them; I just went to the dining hall and ate. I also learned to think and act without being overly concerned about what other people thought of me.

But friendless people can become selfish people. If I had remained on the fringes of friendship, I think I might have become a rather rigid, self-pleasing person who rarely entered the painful grit of someone else's life—and experienced little support in my own painful grit. God, in his kindness, did not allow that to happen. College years brought people able to scramble over the barriers; I tasted the comradery of like-minded people and went out looking for more.

One by one God has broken down my barriers with an appropriate friend at just the right spot. Did I think that committed Christians were blind to intellectual rigors? God blessed my life with Mark Noll. Did I think that wealthy people were mercenary? God sent me "Alice." Did I think that serious Christians lacked creativity? God introduced me to Luci Shaw. Did I think that I could receive wise counsel only from those who shared my faith? God sat me down in Barry's office. Did I think I wanted to give but not receive? God introduced me to grief.

God created us as beings who thrive in the presence of each other. The writer of Ecclesiastes tells us in simple terms, "If one falls down, his friend can help him up." (Independence is great, but some of the tumbles we take in life are more than we can survive alone.) Later the passage adds, "How can one keep warm alone?" (A bed warmed by a spouse who is a friend or a warm cup of tea with a sisterly friend provides physical warmth and emotional comfort.) Proverbs adds, "As iron sharpens iron, so one man sharpens another." (Friendship brings abrasion, even real pain. But as we bump against each other in our conflicts, we rub off those edges that keep us from being all God has designed.) And that design doesn't end with this life. The God who knew us when we were still in our mothers' wombs is creating eternity for us where we will live together with him—as his friends.

The Bible talks about friendship, but it doesn't dwell on the subject. Instead, over and over the Bible shows us examples of friendship in practice. This guide provides an opening study that introduces us to biblical reasons for friendship. Next are five pairs of studies. In each pair, the first study introduces a characteristic of godly friendship; the second lets you look at biblical friends who put that quality to work. Finally, we look at Christ's promised return to earth and our friendship with him that lasts an eternity. At the end of each study is a special feature called "Going Deeper." This reinforces the principles in the study and provides additional biblical material. It can be used on your own or with a group either as a part of the study or between studies.

May this work enrich your relationships here and encourage you about the life to come.

1
Why Friends?

Ecclesiastes 4:1-12

A strange game of alphabet soup plays out in some informal get-acquainted sessions. "I'm an ESFP. How about you?"

"Oh, I'm INFJ."

"Well, at least we have the F in common. Do you cry at sunsets too?"

Myers-Briggs, a test that attempts to measure temperament, has become coffee table talk. The first category of the Myers-Briggs checks out our social orientation. Do I like to spend most of my time with people? Then I'm an extrovert (E). Do I prefer to spend most of my time alone? Then (surprise) I'm an introvert (I).

Extroverts organize their lives around people. Introverts, however, prize time alone and may choose to have fewer friends. But whether we are E's or I's, we need others. Without the benefit of Myers-Briggs, an ancient wisdom writer who was questioning whether anything could bring meaning discovered that friends were among the few worthwhile pursuits in life.

Incidentally, I haven't taken the test, but I suspect that I am an INTJ.

---

1. If you were to rate your need for friendship on a scale of 1 to 10 (ten is high), where would you place yourself? Explain.

What is one of your favorite stories or memories about you and a friend?

2. Read Ecclesiastes 4:1-12. What phrases here help you see the writer's view of the world?

3. What specific complaints does the writer have about society (v. 1)?

about work (vv. 4-6)?

4. Note the number of times the writer says that life is meaningless. Why does he say this?

5. What statements in verses 1-6 do you agree with? Why?

6. If you were a friend to the writer of this text, what would you say to him?

7. Finally, in verses 9-12, the author poses one solution to his despair: a friend. What practical values does he see in friendship?

8. What are some ways that these small practical helps of a friend might dent the despair the writer expressed in verses 1-3?

9. Christian couples often choose the words of verse 12 as a wedding theme: "A cord of three strands is not quickly broken." If two friends (or marriage partners) invite God as the third strand in their cord of friendship, what impact would that have on their relationship?

What impact would a three-stranded cord that included God have on the complaints raised in the earlier section of the chapter?

10. Many people today live with the same despair expressed in Ecclesiastes 4:2-3. Who among your acquaintances needs your friendship? What steps could you make in that direction?

11. Friends are a gift from God. As you pray, mention several of your friends by name and tell God what you appreciate about that person.

Going Deeper
12. The book of Proverbs offers short wise sayings on many subjects—including friendship. Read Proverbs 27:6, 10 and 17. What do you find to be wise in these words?

13. When and how have you experienced one of these sayings to be true?

2
Enjoying Our Differences

1 Corinthians 12:12-31

I once sat in a committee meeting composed of a dozen people of various ages, both genders and a broad range of interests. Our mission was to select the best possible piece of art for a particular purpose. The leader spread out ten choices on a table. We jostled around, looking over each other's shoulders, criticizing this camera angle or that color choice, admiring a facial expression here, a shading in the background there. Finally we narrowed our choices to two and took a vote.

That was when a problem that had been simmering below the surface bubbled to the top. It seemed that several people in the room were employed by one other person present. And none of them dared to vote against the boss. A committee shaped with the purpose of reflecting a variety of perspectives lost its purpose. The boss may have been unconscious of the whole dynamic—or he may have thought he won. But he didn't. Nobody did.

---

1. If you were choosing a church (or a cluster of friends), what similarities to yourself would help you feel comfortable?

What differences from yourself would you accept—or even want? Why?

2. Read 1 Corinthians 12:12-31. Paul opens this section of his letter to the Corinthians by saying, "The body is a unit." What all do you see in this passage that supports that statement?

---

3. Verses 12-19 speak of both unity and diversity. What all unites?

---

4. Who among your circle of friends represents diversity: a foot, a hand, an eye, an ear?

What do you appreciate about each of these people?

---

5. Sometimes when we focus on the ways we are different from other people, our gut feeling is "I do not belong" (v. 15). When and why have you felt this way?

---

6. If your friends accepted the teachings of verses 12-19, what could (or do) they do to help you cope with the feeling of not belonging?

---

7. Focus on verses 21-26. How would you express what Paul is teaching here?

---

8. What situations tempt you to think of someone else, "I don't need you" (v. 21)? (Consider your church or fellowship, business, friends, family.)

9. Focus on verses 22-23. How does Paul tell the Corinthians to deal with people who are "weaker," "less honorable," "unpresentable"?

10. What reasons can you find in verses 24-26 for relating to difficult people in this way?

11. Verse 26 speaks of suffering and honor. When has someone chosen to share your suffering—or when has someone allowed you to share his or her honor?

12. Verses 27-31 speak of how individual differences actually strengthen the church. Describe what you would expect to see in a church where these and other skills were seen as gifts from God to be used for the common good.

13. Look at 1 Corinthians 13:1. Why do you think Paul ends this section about diversity among believers with this question?

14. What do you appreciate about this passage that could help you become a better church member, a better worker, a better family member or a better friend?

Going Deeper
15. Write a letter (or make a phone call) to a friend. Express appreciation for a particular strength that is different from your own.

3
Naomi & Ruth

Ruth 1—2

Family as friends? Family relationships can make "enjoying our differences" a bitter joke.

In a family our differences keep bumping against each other. Besides the obvious differences of age, we also deal with conflicting undercurrents of history and roles. A younger brother feels always shaded by his successful older brother. A daughter knows that she is ready for independence but feels smothered by her mother's anxious concern. A father, feeling a financial crunch, wonders about a second job but knows that he would rarely see his children when they are awake. A college student dreads the routine Sunday afternoon call home, while his mother has been counting the days since Wednesday.

Creating a sense of family is hard. Maintaining it is even harder. Yet many family members, with God's help, overcome incredible odds and, somewhere in adulthood, become friends. Take, for example, two women from the ancient past: Ruth and her mother-in-law, Naomi.

---

1. Describe one family relationship that you have enjoyed.

My Grand mother

---

2. Read Ruth 1—2. What scenes from this story stand out in your mind?

3. What hardships did Ruth and Naomi have to overcome in order to move from a family relationship to a friendship?

4. Study each person's statements about God in the story. How did faith impact the actions of each character?

5. What all did Ruth do to act out the pledge that she made to Naomi in 1:16-17?

6. At the close of the story Naomi's friends described Ruth as "your daughter-in-law who loves you and who is better to you than seven sons" (4:15). Whose friendship has blessed your life in similar ways? How?

7. In what ways did Boaz show himself as a friend to both Ruth and Naomi in chapter 2?

8. In-law relationships are difficult because they combine families with different values, interests and histories. (Ruth was from the country of Moab, ancient enemies of Naomi's people.) How might family differences also enrich potential friendship? (Give some examples.)

9. What's hard about being an in-law? (Consider the roles of parent-in-law, son or daughter-in-law, brother or sister-in-law.)

10. What do you think it would take to be an in-law who is also a friend?

_____

11. Make a list of all your family members. (Include some relatives outside of your immediate family.) Who on this list have you learned to appreciate—in spite of their differences from you? Explain.

_____

12. Which family relationship could be softened by steps toward friendship?

How could you begin those steps?

 Going Deeper
13. Read Ruth 3—4. Notice the negotiations Boaz made with the men at the town gate (4:1-12). What all did he (and they) do to ensure that friendship among them would continue?

_____

14. As they moved toward creating a new family, the characters in the book of Ruth lived out their faith in God in practical, everyday ways. How could you act on your faith in a way that would make you a better present or future family member?

4
Friends in Need
Matthew 25:31-46

A friend in need is a friend indeed," says the English version of an ancient proverb dating as far back as the Greek playwright Euripides. We trill off that proverb with a laugh to cover the minor embarrassment of our need for a car ride home or a forgotten loaf of bread. But what if the need is more serious, a need that tests the ties of friendship? Or what if the person has been needy so long that he or she no longer has friends? Or what if I am not the provider of help, but the person in need? What does God expect of his people when we encounter the harsh face of need?

1. Bring to mind one of your own "needy" times. What is one gesture of help from a friend that stands out in your mind?

Bob opening up his Home to me while I was in the Valley.

2. Read Matthew 25:31-46. Describe the sights and sounds in this scene.

3. What did the people who were present seem to know and not know as they went about their work on earth?

4. What words here express the importance of their works of kindness?

5. Scriptures such as John 3:16 declare that faith in Jesus determines our eternal destiny. How do you reconcile that with what you see in this passage?

6. In this judgment scene, the King describes six needy situations. Picture yourself with one of those needs. What kind of help would you want—and not want?

7. Verse 32 begins by saying that all nations will be gathered. If the people of a country took these six needs (vv. 35-36) as national responsibilities, what actions or policies would you expect to see?

8. What would you expect to see in your own church if it took on the responsibility of meeting those six needs?

9. How might friendship contribute to long-term solutions to the needs mentioned in this text?

10. What risks come to the person who takes on the friendship of someone in need?

11. Think back to some of your own times of need. What did you learn from that experience about appropriate ways to be a "friend in need" to someone else?

Going Deeper
12. Read Luke 10:25-37. Suppose you were to talk with the priest and the Levite about this incident. What do you think each would say in defense of his actions?

13. In view of the entire passage, of what importance was the Samaritan's actions?

14. What suggestions do you have for meeting someone's physical needs without depriving him or her of dignity?

5
David & Mephibosheth

2 Samuel 9; 16:1-4; 19:24-30

David lived in an era when kings killed their competitors. And he'd spent a decade or more on the receiving end of that threat. Saul, the first king of Israel, wanted David dead. David had dodged spears, hidden in caves, even endured Saul's efforts to recruit his wife as a spy. But friendship softened (and complicated) this battle between king and future king. David had sworn eternal friendship to Saul's son Jonathan.

Now Saul was dead and so was Jonathan. David reigned as king. How was David to keep his vow of friendship to Jonathan? If Jonathan had left children, they would be Saul's grandchildren as well—potential heirs to the throne. Political savvy said, "Forget the friendship; wipe them out!"

---

1. Reflect on one of your long-term friendships. When have you had an opportunity to serve your friend in a time of need? (Or when and how has your friend served you?)

---

2. Read 2 Samuel 9. In what practical ways did David show kindness to Mephibosheth? (Draw information from throughout the passage.)

3. Mephibosheth referred to himself in verse 8 as a "dead dog." What can you imagine would be difficult about his situation in that era?

---

4. What did David do that allowed Mephibosheth to maintain a sense of dignity in spite of his needs? (Find all that you can.)

---

5. If you were not able to walk, what kinds of help would you want and not want?

---

6. What did David risk by taking Mephibosheth and Ziba into his household?

---

7. Later David's kingdom suffered an internal rebellion—led by his own son Absalom. King David had to run from Jerusalem to keep from being killed. Just as he left, he met Ziba. Read 2 Samuel 16:1-4. How did Ziba return David's favors?

---

8. How did Ziba explain his presence and Mephibosheth's absence?

---

9. The rebellion ended. Absalom died. David returned, still in power, to the capital city. Read 2 Samuel 19:24-30. How did Mephibosheth's story differ from what Ziba had said?

10. Which story do you think David believed? Explain. (Compare 16:4 with 19:29.)

11. Being a friend to a person in need always involves inconvenience and sometimes real risk. What all might David have lost because of his friendship with Mephibosheth?

12. What inconveniences or risks would come with being a friend to some of the needy people you know?

13. Make a quick list of some of the needy people you know. These might be people with physical, emotional or financial needs, or even people who have special needs because of their life stages—a young mother, an aging relative, a person who has recently experienced grief or divorce.

Select one person from this list that you are willing to offer your friendship. As you consider what this could cost you (time, money, personal risk), what one or two steps can you take to be a friend to this person?

Going Deeper
14. Actually *do* what you have planned in question 13. If you need help, select two or three friends to join you in the project. Pray regularly for the person you are serving. Keep journal notes of the events. Look for ways that God is at work. Note any changes you see in yourself.

Deb & Rob, Rick & wife, Dwight in VAncouver

6
Forgiving Friends
Matthew 18:12-35

Last summer I hiked a section of Lake Superior's north shore. Most of my companions were followers of New Age teachings. We held in common a love for experiencing nature close-up, but conversations along the trail challenged my thinking in unexpected ways. One day, for example, I stumbled and bumped into an elderly man. "Oh, I'm sorry," I apologized.

"You should learn to stop saying that," he said. "You did nothing wrong—there is no right and there is no wrong. So stop weighing yourself with false guilt and apologies." I must say it was a bit unnerving to hear words of such moral emptiness, not from a teen in temporary rebellion but from a gentleman a full generation my senior.

"But I like being able to say 'I'm sorry,'" I finally sputtered. "Those words prevent misunderstanding. You might have thought I was trying to knock you down! Besides, even if I intended to harm you, 'I'm sorry' opens the possibility of forgiveness and a fresh start."

He chuckled but was, I think, unconvinced. Yet in my experience, friends—if they are to remain friends—need to practice forgiveness.

---

1. When has forgiveness (or lack of it) impacted one of your friendships?

2. Read Matthew 18:12-20. Jesus tells of two different situations in these verses. What is your emotional response to each? Explain.

3. What similarities can you find between the parable of the sheep and Christ's instructions about a brother who sins?

Sins lost sheep,
one found wanting to
Be foond

4. Study the four opportunities for reconciliation presented to the person who sins (vv. 15-17). What is difficult about each step?

Confrontation

5. Notice that the goal of this procedure, according to verse 15, is that you may win your brother over. How might each of these steps help a person not to wander farther from God?

6. In verse 21 Peter follows the teachings about attempting to reconcile with people who wander by asking a logical next question, "How many times shall I forgive my brother?" What is risky about trying to forgive someone who has hurt you?

7. Read Matthew 18:21-35. Study the two examples of debt collection described here. Find all the similarities that you can (vv. 23-30).

8. What differences do you see?

9. In the first half of the servant parable, the amount owed is a large sum of money. Ten thousand talents represented the highest Greek number combined with the largest Roman unit of money. What does this suggest about the nature of our sin debt to God and the extent of God's forgiveness?

10. What all do you see in verses 31-35 that shows how the master viewed unforgiveness in his servants?

11. Bring to mind a person that you have had trouble forgiving. In a brief time of silence, ask God's forgiveness for your own lack of forgiveness.

12. What is one way that you could demonstrate your desire to forgive this person? *My active drug my family to use in past hurt others to*

Going Deeper

13. Read Matthew 16:16-20. Jesus promised that Peter would have a position of great responsibility in the coming church. In view of Matthew 18:35 and the parable it summarizes, what all do you think Peter would say to future Christians who asked him, "How many times shall I forgive my brother?"

14. Take a few moments to meditate on your own sins—past and present. What has God forgiven you? (Be as specific as is appropriate for your setting.)

7
A Father & His Son

Luke 15:11-32

W hy don't you treat me like you treat your friends?" complained a teenager to her mother. The mother cringed—but only for a moment.

"My friends don't treat me like trash," she shot back. "My friends answer when I say, 'Good morning.' They appreciate my cooking. They tell me that I look nice. They don't yell at me. They listen to what I say. And they don't keep me waiting up for them all night!"

But even as she spoke, this hassled mom pictured loving past and future images of her child: at birth, taking her first steps, marching off to kindergarten, dressing for her first date, packing for her first year of college, walking down the aisle in a wedding gown, handing her a grandchild. Family living brings out our best qualities, but it also reveals our worst. Forgiveness helps.

---

1. Recall a time during your growing-up years when you had a fight or serious disagreement with a brother, sister or other family member. What did you fight about and why?

What did this event reveal about each of you?

2. Read Luke 15:11-32. Who in this story is most like you? Explain.

3. Beginning at the beginning, tell this story in your own words—as if you were the youngest son.

4. What do you think the older son would say about his brother's version of the story?

5. Family forgiveness plays a major part in this story. Focus on each member of the family one at a time. What did each have to forgive in the other two family members?

6. What all did the father do to help the brothers forgive each other?

7. In what ways does the father in this story remind you of God?

8. Glance through this story one more time. If you were to write a continuation that begins five years later, what would you write?

9. If you were the father in this family, what would you want to see five years later?

10. What forgiveness do you hope to see in your own family in the next five years?

11. What one or two steps could you take that might lead toward that forgiveness?

12. Forgiveness can sometimes lead to friendship, but not always. Do you think that it is possible for parents and their children ever to become real friends? Explain.

13. For what do you personally need to forgive a parent, child or sibling? (Or what does one of them need to forgive you for?)

Going Deeper
14. Who within your extended family feels most like a friend? Describe your relationship.

15. How can you continue to nurture that relationship toward friendship?

8
Loving Friends

1 John 4:7-21

In *The Four Loves,* C. S. Lewis contrasts friendship love with other forms of love: "Lovers are normally face to face, absorbed in each other," writes Lewis; "friends side by side, absorbed in some common interest." And later: "The typical expression of opening friendship would be something like, 'What? You too? I thought I was the only one.' "

But even as Lewis attempts to distinguish one form of love from another, in his final chapter on charity love, Lewis admits to a common origin of all good forms of love: "When we see the face of God we shall know that we have always known it. He has been a party to, has made, sustained and moved moment by moment within, all our earthly experiences of innocent love. All that was true love in them was, even on earth, far more His than ours, and ours only because His."

It seems that God loves us—as a gift. But he also gives us the gift of love—for each other, for himself. The love of friends is one of those love gifts from God.

---

1. Who was your best friend during your growing-up years? How did you and your friend show that you cared about each other?

---

2. Read 1 John 4:7-21. Six times in this letter (twice in this passage) John uses the phrase "Dear friends." Would you want to be a friend to a person who could write this kind of letter? Why or why not?

3. John uses the word *love* 27 times in this short section of his letter. What all does he teach us here about God's love?

4. Verse 19 says, "We love because he first loved us." According to this passage, what impact should God's love have on our own attempts to love? (Find all that you can.)

5. What all would you expect to see in a person who tried to imitate the love of God as it is described here?

6. Why do you think John draws such a strong link between loving God and loving each other?

7. Verse 10 describes God's love as an "atoning sacrifice." What sacrifices have various people made in their love for you?

8. What kinds of sacrifices has your love for someone else required?

9. Verse 16 says, "God is love." How is that different from saying, "Love is God"?

10. Verse 18 says, "There is no fear in love. But perfect love drives out fear." Why are love and fear sometimes mixed in our human forms of love?

11. As you think through love as it is described in this passage, what are you particularly thankful for?

12. When has a friend offered you some aspect of love as it is described in this passage?

13. What current relationship would you like to enrich by bringing some of the ingredients of love described here?

How can you begin that process?

Going Deeper
14. Read 1 John 3:1-10. Picture yourself as a child of God hearing these words of love for you. Thank him for what he offers you in these verses. Offer your own love in return.

9
Jesus with Mary, Martha & Lazarus

John 11:1-44; 12:1-11

It's lonely at the top. Corporate executives, political heads of state, even pastors of churches have trouble making friends—at least with those who are not their peers. Friendship demands a certain vulnerability that is expensive to those whose position demands that they take charge of situations. Even wealth can become a barrier to friendship. As one wealthy person said, "I never know who my real friends are."

It's also lonely at the bottom. Other people don't want to take the risk of knowing about overwhelming needs. That knowledge creates a double-bind: expensive to meet the needs and guilt-producing to ignore them. The comfortable choice is to avoid contact.

Imagine the potential isolation of the Son of God. He was Ruler of the Universe, yet he chose the company of a dozen tradesmen as disciples. He also participated in a loving friendship with a little family in Bethany.

1. If you could have any person in the world as your friend—regardless of that person's position—who would you choose? Why?

2. Read John 11:1-44 and 12:1-11. How did people here show their love for each other? (Find all that you can.)

3. John 11:5-6 says, "Jesus loved Martha and her sister and Lazarus. Yet when he heard that Lazarus was sick, he stayed where he was two more days." Why? (Use the rest of the story to explain.)

4. Friends often hesitate to ask personal questions about faith—especially during a time of crisis. Yet in 11:26, Jesus asked Martha a very pointed question. How might your own answer to this question affect the way you think you would cope with illness or death?

5. Do you think that Lazarus still considered Jesus his friend by the end of this account? Explain.

6. In John 11:4 and 40 Jesus mentions the glory of God. What do you see of God's glory through the events of this story?

7. Focus on John 12:1-11. At this time Jesus was one week away from his own death. In what ways might the events here help these friends prepare for the coming ordeal?

8. What would you hope to receive from your own friends during a time of serious loss?

9. As you think through Christ's friendship with the Bethany family, what patterns would you like to bring to your own friendships?

10. What is one way that you could express love to a friend in the coming week?

Going Deeper
11. Read Luke 10:38-42. Notice what each person said and did. What do the words and actions here tell you about the relationship each of these people had with the others?

12. In verse 42 Jesus said that Mary had chosen what "will not be taken away from her." How might Christ's praise of Mary help you decide what you do with the time you have for your own friends?

10
Friends Accountable to Friends

Galatians 6:1-10

My daughter was dead in a car wreck and so was her unborn child. In the next few weeks, as I tried to put together my fractured life, I realized that I faced the greatest challenge to my faith that I had ever known. "I don't want to become a spiritual cripple over this," I said.

So I called a friend, Mary. We agreed that if I did not call her by Friday of each week, she would call me. She would ask me certain questions about how I was practicing my faith. She would hear my questions about God. She would pray for me and with me.

This process was not without risk—especially for Mary. We discussed these risks. Did she have the time and energy this six-month commitment would demand? Was she emotionally stable enough to cry with me, but not be overwhelmed by my grief? Was she steady enough in her own faith to hear the angry questions I would hurl at God?

My continued faith is testimony to her good work (along with the love and prayers of many other believing friends). Years later, I helped her through a tough patch of her own. It's the nature of Christian friendship. We keep each other accountable.

---

1. If you were making a report on your spiritual progress during the past week, what would you say? (Include at least one positive item and one area where you would like to improve.)

2. Read Galatians 6:1-10. What attitudes are Christians to have when they help each other in these various ways? (Try to find something in almost every verse.)

_____

3. If you were to live with a group of Christians who function in the way described here, what responsibilities would you expect to have?

What would you expect others to do for you?

_____

4. Verse 1 gives particular responsibilities to "you who are spiritual." What words of caution do you find in the rest of the passage?

_____

5. Why do you think we must be so careful when we try to help someone else get straightened out?

_____

6. Verse 2 says that we are to carry each other's burdens, yet verse 5 says that we should carry our own loads. Why might a responsible Christian expect to do both of these—depending on the circumstances?

_____

7. What kinds of situations might lead you to ask a Christian friend for spiritual guidance?

8. What would be hard about letting someone check up on your spiritual progress?

9. Focus on verse 6. What "give and take" between believers does this verse suggest?

10. In verses 7-10 Paul speaks several times of sowing and reaping. What personal encouragement do you find here?

11. What are some ways that friends can help each other to continue in faith?

12. Consider again your response to question 1. If you were to report on your spiritual progress in the week to come, what would you want a friend to ask you at the end of that time?

Going Deeper

13. Verse 2 says that when we carry each other's burdens we fulfill "the law of Christ." We can't be sure which specific law Paul meant, but several statements from Christ may help us. Read Matthew 5:43-44; 7:12; Mark 12:30-31 and Galatians 5:14. If you wanted to help someone through a time of spiritual difficulties, what help would you find in these laws that Christ gave?

14. What help do these laws give you as you look to the week ahead?

11
David & Nathan
2 Samuel 11:1—12:25

I've met someone else," said the soft voice on the phone. "I've left the house; I thought you'd want to know."

I felt as stunned as if I had been jolted by an electric current. Our families had been friends for a quarter of a century. We'd had babies at the same time, taken vacations together, attended each other's family funerals. He was a leader in his church, the spiritual patriarch of his extended family. When our marriage had been at a shaky point, our friend had come to help us patch things up. Now his marriage was at an end—or seemed to be. And maybe his walk with God as well. What were we to do, if anything?

1. What kinds of situations have led you to wonder if a friend ought to step in and point out what is wrong?

2. Read 2 Samuel 11. What bothers you about David's actions in this story?

3. Why do you think Uriah would not go home (vv. 7-13)?

4. What do Joab's actions (vv. 14-21) say about his character?

5. If you had been Bathsheba's friend, what would you worry about?

6. If you had been David's friend, what (if anything) would you say to him?

7. This chapter ends with the terse statement "But the thing David had done displeased the LORD." Read 2 Samuel 12:1-25. What connections do you see between Nathan's parable of verses 1-4 and David's actions in the previous chapter?

8. Study Nathan's description of David's life in verses 7-9. What perspective did Nathan offer that David may not have seen (or wanted to see) until this point?

9. Once David recognized his sin (v. 13), how did he express his faith?

10. How do you think this story would have ended differently if Nathan had refused to confront David with what he had done wrong?

11. Accountability among friends will at times lead to confrontation, and friendship may not survive this. What measures can we take in friendship that could make healthy confrontation possible?

Going Deeper
12. As you observe God in this story, what warnings do you find in regard to your own actions? (Be as specific as you can.)

13. In the closing scene of this story, God sends Nathan back to David one more time, where he names David and Bathsheba's newborn son Jedidiah, meaning "loved by God." What comfort does this scene offer you about your own life and the lives of your friends?

12
Forever Friends
1 Thessalonians 4:13—5:11

It was fun seeing them together at the wedding. My friend Agnes (mother of the bride) had often spoken of her friend Barbara Ann. She and Barbara Ann had grown up together. They'd attended the same parochial school for girls; at day's end, they would march out of school side-by-side in their identical uniforms. As soon as they were off the school grounds, they'd roll their long socks down to their ankles and pull tangee lipstick out of their pockets, giggling at their brave worldliness. Agnes, always full of adventure, declares that Barbara Ann alone kept her from crossing the invisible line that would get her kicked out of school.

Barbara Ann and Agnes each married young, moved to different parts of the country, and raised a houseful of children—a pattern that would end most friendships. But frequent visits and phone calls full of intimate talk kept them close. At the wedding, I felt that I was meeting a long-absent member of the family. Agnes and Barbara Ann stood arm in arm, as alike as sisters. Barbara Ann's efficient movements around the fringes of the activity tied up the loose edges endemic to weddings; her quiet words steadied the bride—and her mother. I was glad that God created these two women, even from childhood, as a gift to each other.

---

1. Describe one of your long-standing friendships. (Who is it with? How did you meet? Why and how did you remain friends?)

2. Read 1 Thessalonians 4:13-18. What visual images does this passage present?

3. Paul begins this passage by saying that Christians do not grieve like people who have no hope. What part does Christ play in the hope offered here?

4. Paul ends this passage by saying, "Therefore encourage each other with these words." What do you find encouraging in these verses?

5. Try to picture yourself with a dear friend (even one who has died) alive together in the scene described here. What images and feelings come to your mind?

6. Read 1 Thessalonians 5:1-11. What words and phrases suggest warning?

7. Paul speaks here of two kinds of people, those who belong to darkness and those who belong to light. How, according to the text, are these people different from each other?

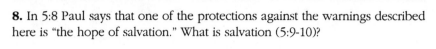

8. In 5:8 Paul says that one of the protections against the warnings described here is "the hope of salvation." What is salvation (5:9-10)?

Why is it a hope?

_____

9. In view of the warnings and the promise here, what would you encourage a friend to do or to be?

_____

10. First Thessalonians 4:17 tells us that we will be "with the Lord forever," and 5:10 adds that we will "live together with him." If some of your friendships are in fact eternal relationships, how might that effect the way you conduct them now?

_____

11. Use this passage as an outline for prayer. Thank God for what he offers you throughout these verses.

Going Deeper
12. During your twelve studies on friendship, you have thought of many of your friends—past and present. Now mention the names of your friends one by one in prayer. Thank God for a special quality that you enjoy in each one.

Leader's Notes

Leading a Bible discussion can be an enjoyable and rewarding experience. But it can also be *scary*—especially if you've never done it before. If this is your feeling, you're in good company. When God asked Moses to lead the Israelites out of Egypt, he replied, "O Lord, please send someone else to do it!" (Ex 4:13).

When Solomon became king of Israel, he felt the task was beyond his abilities. "I am only a little child and do not know how to carry out my duties. . . . Who is able to govern this great people of yours?" (1 Kings 3:7, 9).

When God called Jeremiah to be a prophet, he replied, "Ah, Sovereign LORD, . . . I do not know how to speak; I am only a child" (Jer 1:6).

The list goes on. The apostles were "unschooled, ordinary men" (Acts 4:13). Timothy was young, frail and frightened. Paul's "thorn in the flesh" made him feel weak. But God's response to all of his servants—including you—is essentially the same: "My grace is sufficient for you" (2 Cor 12:9). Relax. God helped these people in spite of their weaknesses, and he can help you in spite of your feelings of inadequacy.

There is another reason why you should feel encouraged. Leading a Bible discussion is not difficult if you follow certain guidelines. You don't need to be an expert on the Bible or a trained teacher. The suggestions listed below should enable you to effectively and enjoyably fulfill your role as leader.

Preparing to Lead

1. Ask God to help you understand and apply the passage to your own life. Unless this happens, you will not be prepared to lead others. Pray too for the various members of the group. Ask God to give you an enjoyable and profitable time together studying his Word.

2. As you begin each study, read and reread the assigned Bible passage to familiarize yourself with what the author is saying. In the case of book studies, you may want to read through the entire book prior to the first study. This will give you a helpful overview of its contents.

3. This study guide is based on the New International Version of the Bible. It will help you and the group if you use this translation as the basis for your study and discussion. Encourage others to use the NIV also, but allow them the freedom to use whatever translation they prefer.

4. Carefully work through each question in the study. Spend time in meditation and reflection as you formulate your answers.

5. Write your answers in the space provided in the study guide. This will help you to express your understanding of the passage clearly.

6. It might help you to have a Bible dictionary handy. Use it to look up any unfamiliar words, names or places. (For additional help on how to study a passage, see chapter five of *Leading Bible Discussions,* IVP.)

7. Once you have finished your own study of the passage, familiarize yourself with the leader's notes for the study you are leading. These are designed to help you in several ways. First, they tell you the purpose the study guide author had in mind while writing the study. Take time to think through how the study questions work together to accomplish that purpose. Second, the notes provide you with additional background information or comments on some of the questions. This information can be useful if people have difficulty understanding or answering a question. Third, the leader's notes can alert you to potential problems you may encounter during the study.

8. If you wish to remind yourself of anything mentioned in the leader's notes, make a note to yourself below that question in the study.

Leading the Study

1. Begin the study on time. Unless you are leading an evangelistic Bible study, open with prayer, asking God to help you to understand and apply the passage.

2. Be sure that everyone in your group has a study guide. Encourage them to prepare beforehand for each discussion by working through the questions in the guide.

3. At the beginning of your first time together, explain that these studies are meant to be discussions not lectures. Encourage the members of the group to participate. However, do not put pressure on those who may be hesitant to speak during the first few sessions.

4. Read the introductory paragraph at the beginning of the discussion. This will orient the group to the passage being studied.

5. Read the passage aloud if you are studying one chapter or less. You may choose to do this yourself, or someone else may read if he or she has been asked to do so prior to the study. Longer passages may occasionally be read in parts at different times during the study. Some studies may cover several chapters. In such cases reading aloud would probably take too much time, so the group members should simply read the assigned passages prior to the study.

6. As you begin to ask the questions in the guide, keep several things in mind. First, the questions are designed to be used just as they are written. If you wish, you may simply read them aloud to the group. Or you may prefer to express them in your own words. However, unnecessary rewording of the questions is not recommended.

Second, the questions are intended to guide the group toward understanding and applying the *main idea* of the passage. The author of the guide has stated his or her view of this central idea in the *purpose* of the study in the leader's notes. You should try to understand how the passage expresses this idea and how the study questions work together to lead the group in that direction.

There may be times when it is appropriate to deviate from the study guide. For example, a question may have already been answered. If so, move on to the next question. Or someone may raise an important question not covered in the guide. Take time to discuss it! The important thing is to use discretion. There may be many routes you can travel to reach the goal of the study. But the easiest route is usually the one the author has suggested.

7. Avoid answering your own questions. If necessary, repeat or rephrase them until they are clearly understood. An eager group quickly becomes passive and silent if they think the leader will do most of the talking.

8. Don't be afraid of silence. People may need time to think about the question before formulating their answers.

9. Don't be content with just one answer. Ask, "What do the rest of you think?" or "Anything else?" until several people have given answers to the question.

10. Acknowledge all contributions. Try to be affirming whenever possible. Never reject an answer. If it is clearly wrong, ask, "Which verse led you to that conclusion?" or again, "What do the rest of you think?"

11. Don't expect every answer to be addressed to you, even though this will probably happen at first. As group members become more at ease, they will begin to truly interact with each other. This is one sign of a healthy discussion.

12. Don't be afraid of controversy. It can be very stimulating. If you don't resolve an issue completely, don't be frustrated. Move on and keep it in mind for later. A subsequent study may solve the problem.

13. Stick to the passage under consideration. It should be the source for answering the questions. Discourage the group from unnecessary cross-referencing. Likewise, stick to the subject and avoid going off on tangents.

14. Periodically summarize what the *group* has said about the passage. This helps to draw together the various ideas mentioned and gives continuity to the study. But don't preach.

15. Conclude your time together with conversational prayer. Be sure to ask God's help to apply those things which you learned in the study.

16. End on time.

Many more suggestions and helps are found in *Leading Bible Discussions* (IVP). Reading and studying through that would be well worth your time.

Components of Small Groups

A healthy small group should do more than study the Bible. There are four components you should consider as you structure your time together.

Nurture. Being a part of a small group should be a nurturing and edifying experience. You should grow in your knowledge and love of God and each other. If we are to properly love God, we must know and keep his commandments (Jn 14:15). That is why Bible study should be a foundational part of your small group. But you can be nurtured by other things as well. You can memorize Scripture, read and discuss a book, or occasionally listen to a tape of a good speaker.

Community. Most people have a need for close friendships. Your small group can be an excellent place to cultivate such relationships. Allow time for informal interaction before and after the study. Have a time of sharing during the meeting. Do fun things together as a group, such as a potluck supper or a picnic. Have someone bring refreshments to the meeting. Be creative!

Worship. A portion of your time together can be spent in worship and prayer. Praise God together for who he is. Thank him for what he has done and is doing in your lives and in the world. Pray for each other's needs. Ask God to help you to apply what you have learned. Sing hymns together.

Mission. Many small groups decide to work together in some form of outreach. This can be a practical way of applying what you have learned. You can host a series of evangelistic discussions for your friends or neighbors. You can visit people at a home for the elderly. Help a widow with cleaning or repair jobs around her home. Such projects can have a transforming influence on your group.

For a detailed discussion of the nature and function of small groups, read *Small Group Leaders' Handbook* or *The Big Book on Small Groups* (both from IVP).

Study 1. Why Friends? Ecclesiastes 4:1-12.

Purpose: To appreciate God's gift of friendship with other people and with himself.

Question 1. Use the first question to involve each person present. A simple number rating is fine. Those who wish to make explanation may do so. Then move into the second question and allow time for several brief stories. Be ready with a short (not too spectacular) one of your own. Be aware that even people who consider themselves introverts may have a great need for friendship. And their friendships may be more intense than those who prefer large numbers of friends at a more shallow level.

Every study begins with an "approach" question, which is meant to be asked before the passage is read. These questions are important for several reasons.

First, they help the group to warm up to each other. No matter how well a group may know each other, there is always a stiffness that needs to be overcome before people will begin to talk openly. A good question will break the ice.

Second, approach questions get people thinking along the lines of the topic of the study. Most people will have lots of different things going on in their minds (dinner, an important meeting coming up, how to get the car fixed) that will have nothing to do with the study. A creative question will get their attention and draw them into the discussion.

Third, approach questions can reveal where our thoughts or feelings need to be transformed by Scripture. That is why it is especially important not to read the passage before the approach question is asked. The passage will tend to color the honest reactions people would otherwise give because they are, of course, supposed to think the way the Bible does. Giving honest responses before they find out what the Bible says may help them see where their thoughts or attitudes need to be changed.

Question 2. Use this question to help your group gain an overview of this section of the text. People should point out phrases in almost every verse. If your group has trouble responding to such a comprehensive question, try breaking it down. Ask: Do you see the tone of this passage as optimistic, pessimistic or realistic? What words and phrases in the text cause you to think that?

Question 4. Your group should point out that the man was alone, that wealth did not bring contentment—perhaps because he had no one to share it with and seemed unable to experience joy (v. 8).

Question 5. Verses 1-6 express a variety of complaints, observations and even a suggestion or two. Most of us can identify with one or more of the statements. Use this question to help group members understand each other's perspective.

Question 6. Encourage people to respond to the author of Ecclesiastes as if he were a friend. Many of us have friends with these complaints. Some of the complaints are our own. Some will agree with this "friend." Others will offer compassion and hope. In this way group members can minister indirectly to each other. They will also gain resources to share with similar friends.

Question 11. You can use this question in a couple of ways. At the beginning you can suggest that people tell each other what they appreciate about their various friends (including, perhaps, people in the group). But then remind them that friends are, in fact, a gift from God. So close your time together by offering prayers of thanks as suggested in the question.

Questions 12-13. "Going deeper" sections provide additional material related to each study. You can use these sections by working them into the midsection of the discussion, by adding them at the close of the study or suggesting it as a personal follow-up to the group meeting.

Study 2. Enjoying Our Differences. 1 Corinthians 12:12-31.

Purpose: To respect and draw on the differences that God has created among his people.

Question 2. Use this question to gain a broad understanding of the passage. Your group should find answers in almost every verse. There is no need to be thorough at this point; you will cover these sources of unity with more depth later in the study.

Question 4. Help members of your group to first understand what a foot, hand, eye or ear might do, then to name people who especially demonstrate those qualities. For example, a "foot" might be one who is quick to jump in and *do* something. An "ear" might be a person who listens with wisdom, compassion and understanding. If some people name others in the group, the question will help you to express appreciation for each other in a way that reflects the teachings of the passage.

Question 9. Your group should discuss the acceptance and protection expressed in the words *indispensable, special honor* and *modesty*. If you have time for a follow-up question at this point, ask: "How is Paul's approach toward difficult people different from normal practice?"

Question 10. Your group should study such phrases as "God has combined" (v. 24), "so that there should be no division" (v. 25), "equal concern for each other" (v. 25). People should also look at the prospect of suffering and rejoicing together (v. 26).

Question 14. If your group does not move automatically into discussing practical ways to put these observations to work, ask: What is one step you could take toward meeting that challenge?

Study 3. Naomi & Ruth. Ruth 1—2.

Purpose: To allow our faith in God to grow us into people who have the ability to become friends with members of our families.

Question 3. Your group should find a variety of hardships as they survey the story. These include: cultural differences (1:2; 2:10), death (1:3, 5), lack of grandchildren (1:5), poverty (1:6; 2:3), bitterness (1:20), danger (2:9), differing homelands (2:10), rival parents (2:11), shared housing (2:23), and unfamiliar customs (2:2-3).

Question 4. Naomi's references to God occur in 1:20-21 and 2:20. Ruth speaks of God in 1:16-18. Boaz mentions God in 2:4, 12. Later in the story, the town elders call on God in 4:11-12 as do Naomi's friends in 4:14-15. As your group members spot each reference, ask that they link the beliefs (implied or stated) with the actions.

Question 5. Your group should outline Ruth's actions in chapter 2.

Question 7. The following references may help: 2:4, 8-12, 14-16.

Questions 11-12. Allow a few moments for people to pencil a list of family members. Then conduct a discussion of these two questions with all of the sensitivity you can muster. (Family relationships are often tense and painful.) Be aware that not everyone will want to speak, and that some family relationships are not within our power to repair.

Study 4. Friends in Need. Matthew 25:31-46.

Purpose: To express friendship by giving and receiving in times of need.

Question 1. Encourage each person to tell a brief story of personal experience in response to this question. You will refer to it again at the close of the session.

Question 3. The people of this scene seemed to be aware of the needy around them on earth, but neither group of people knew that the needy represented Christ himself. (See verses 37 and 44.)

Question 4. Your group should point out such words and phrases as: "throne" and "heavenly glory" (v. 31), "separate" (v. 32), "inheritance" and "kingdom" (v. 34), "depart," "cursed," "devil," "eternal fire,"(v. 41), "eternal punishment" and "eternal life" (v. 46). As they point out these words, they should also discuss their meaning and significance.

Question 5. This may be a difficult question, especially for those who feel that they must earn God's favor in order to inherit eternal life. First John 3:17-19 may be of some help here. It expresses the concept that true faith in Jesus reveals itself in loving service. We do not earn our way to heaven, but if we are not helping those in need, we ought to question whether our faith in Jesus is genuine.

Question 6. The six needs are mentioned in verses 35-36. Use this question to let people mentally take the difficult position of the needy person. (It is often easier to give than receive.) In order to explore the array of situations described in the text, try to get at least one response regarding each of the six needs.

Question 11. Remind your group of some of the stories told in the first question—or perhaps other relevant memories of need have surfaced by now. Ask that people build on these experiences as well as information from the text to discuss appropriate ways to help others.

Question 13. Your group should note some obvious importance to the injured man. But careful scrutiny of the text should also reveal that this story was, in fact, a response to the question of Luke 10:25, "What must I do to inherit eternal life?"

Study 5. David & Mephibosheth. 2 Samuel 9; 16:1-14; 19:24-30.

Purpose: To realistically assess the risk of becoming a friend to a needy person and to take that risk.

Question 1. No one lives a trouble-free life. In long-term friendships, one or both members will have experienced need. Help the group to discuss ways that they have served each other during those times. This question should help your group move into the area of need. It will build on the previous study and prepare them to look at the risks David endured because of his commitment to friendship with Jonathan—and therefore with Jonathan's son.

Question 3. For the story of how Mephibosheth became crippled see 2 Samuel 4:1-4.

Question 4. If the group is slow to catch the implications of David's help, ask these follow-up questions: "Why do you think that David included Ziba in his help to Mephibosheth?" "Why did he restore Saul's land to Mephibosheth?" "What did Mephibosheth gain by eating at David's table?"

Answers to these questions should show that David provided a means for Mephibosheth to maintain independence, economic security and dignity. By seating him at the king's table, David gave Mephibosheth respect, not to mention adequate diet. (Eating at David's table also allowed surveillance, not an unwise decision in view of the events that followed.)

Question 5. Dependence and independence are in constant tension for people unable to walk. So is dignity. Use this question to allow group members to mentally put themselves in a wheelchair. What kinds of help would allow them to keep some sense of independence and dignity?

Question 6. In answering this question, consider the obvious personal and economic risks, but also the political risks reflected in the introduction to this study. In addition, David had some of the same reasons to fear helping Mephibosheth that we fear in our own contacts with people who are needy.

Someone will probably notice the last sentence of verse 10. Ziba's household was no small force of able-bodied men. David must have wondered if he could count on their loyalty—and what might happen to him if they turned against him.

Question 10. Let your group discuss reactions to David's decision. Some may think that Mephiboseth, a "Johnny-come-lately," should have lost his share of the inheritance. Others may say that Ziba was lying and should have been banished. Still others may agree with David. He couldn't know who was telling the truth, so he was right in dividing the property between them.

Question 11. If you have covered potential answers already, just do a quick recap at this stage. David did give up property and food. He may have lost respect among strong loyalists who viewed his kindness to Saul's son as unnecessary risk. He might have harbored a traitor and a spy at his own table. He could have lost his kingdom and his life. Even without that, he probably lost his ability to trust either Mephibosheth or Ziba. Still he kept them on as friends and tenants.

Question 12. This is not a spot for quick-fix answers. Many of us avoid real contact with needy people because we don't want to take the risks their needs create—but we don't like that quality in ourselves. So we house ourselves within barriers by where we choose to work, live, even where we go to church, so that we do not have to see people with serious needs. These barriers protect us not only from inconvenience, but also from recognizing our own selfishness. Use this question to take an honest look at some potential risks—even if it is as simple as time taken away from work in order to visit an aging uncle on the way home. Weighing the cost of being a friend to someone in need will help us make realistic decisions about what we are willing to offer.

Question 13. Pause after the first stage of this question to allow time for people to write a list of names and needs. Allow enough silent time for thoughtful consideration. Then invite concrete steps (even small ones) from each person.

Study 6. Forgiving Friends. Matthew 18:12-35.

Purpose: To forgive our friends in the same way that Christ has forgiven us.

Question 1. This may be a difficult question for a group to answer at the opening of a study. Yet a couple of brief stories about friends and forgiveness will prepare the group to receive the biblical text at a personal level. If responses are slow, lead the way by giving a short, but not too impressive, example from your own experience.

Question 2. Encourage brief answers here that reflect an emotional response to each story. Most people will see the parable of the sheep in warm, positive tones and the instructions about church discipline as harsh and punitive. Just accept the initial reactions at this point. As the study progresses, your group may begin to see that these two events are quite similar in purpose.

Question 3. Encourage your group to linger long enough on this question to discover several similarities between the two stories. People should notice that both deal with a wanderer, both have the shepherd/brother going to great effort to bring the wanderer back, both show results of the wanderer's return (or loss) in heaven, both speak of celebration if the lost one returns, both show the great value God holds for the sheep/person who wanders.

Question 5. Possible reconciliation is fairly obvious in the first three steps, and your group should discuss ways this might occur during the course of each step. But people may have trouble seeing how treating someone as "a pagan or a tax collector" could lead toward return to faith.

Jesus may have used this phrase because it was a common synonym in Jewish culture for excommunication. But we must also consider how Jesus himself treated pagans and tax collectors. He healed them (the daughter of the Canaanite woman in Mt 15:21-28), he ate with them (Zacchaeus in Lk 19:1-10), he even called one to become his disciple (Matthew [Levi]—in Mk 2:13-17). So Jesus may have intended that we treat this persistent wanderer with all the kindness (and wariness) that we would treat any outsider we wished to win to faith.

In addition, we must also keep in mind the teachings of Paul in 1 Corinthians 5:1-5 where a person who practiced sexual immorality was to be expelled (temporarily) from the congregation so that "the sinful nature may be destroyed and his spirit saved on the day of the Lord."

If you want to analyze this passage further, ask, "How do the words of verses 18-19 give importance to the process described in verses 15-17?" Verse 18 is quite similar to Christ's words to Peter in 16:19. Though we may not know exactly what Jesus meant, we can know that he imparted a strong power on the church when it deals with people who might wander from faith. Matthew 18:19-20 is often misused as a recipe for getting what we want from God when we pray. The context, however, assumes a situation of church discipline. It also assumes that prayers "in my name" ask what Jesus himself would give if he were present.

Question 6. This question will begin to lead your group into the area of past hurts and forgiveness. It will help at the outset to talk about the real risks involved. You will be discussing this area at a more personal level before the study is over.

Question 10. Encourage your group to pick out relevant words and phrases from verses 32-35. Obviously God takes unwillingness to forgive quite seriously.

Questions 11-12. Conduct a time of meditation and prayer following question 13. Then ask each person who is willing to respond to question 14. Be sensitive to the hurt these questions may reveal. If it seems appropriate, close with a time of praying for each other that God will heal the pain of these relationships as a first step toward peace and forgiveness.

Question 13. Use this question to help your group summarize all the teachings of this passage. Don't settle for surface answers. Your group should stress the relationship between Christ's forgiveness of us and our ability/obligation to forgive others. You should also emphasize the importance of reconciliation in God's eyes. If time permits you can draw all three stories of the passage together by asking: What connections do you see between a shepherd's care for the sheep that strays (vv. 12-14), the care of a church for a brother who sins (vv. 15-20), and our own forgiveness to a person who has harmed us (vv. 21-35)? Be sure to leave time for the two personal application questions that follow.

Question 14. Do not encourage "confessions" that people might later regret—particularly if they involve others who are not present. On the other hand, sins that are too general may not provide an adequate sense of God's specific forgiveness—and therefore a basis for our own power to forgive. Appropriate samples might include: God has forgiven me for not being a perfect parent, or even the parent that I could have been. God has forgiven me for selfishness—which I still am trying to conquer. God has forgiven me for an angry fight I had with my brother when I was thirteen. If this question seems too personal for the trust level within your group, try an alternate:

What do you especially appreciate about God's forgiveness?

Study 7. A Father & His Son. Luke 15:11-32.

Purpose: To practice forgiveness as one means of creating friendship with our families.

Question 1. Encourage a rather lighthearted time of childhood storytelling. The second part of the question may help people gain some perspective on these events as they helped define and perhaps shape their current characters.

Question 2. Characters in the story include the father, the older son, the younger son and the party guests.

Question 3. Suggest that half of the group listen to the story as if they were the younger son. The other half can listen through the ears of the older son.

Question 5. If your group needs a breakdown of this question, ask: What did the father have to forgive each son (vv. 12, 13, 14, 25, 28, 30)? What did each son have to forgive his father? (The younger son probably had to forgive the father for whatever reasons caused him to leave home in the first place. Regarding the older son, see verses 20, 29, 30.) What did the sons have to forgive each other? (Answers will be similar to those transgressions against the father, except they will appear from the perspective of a brother, who might sustain his own personal losses because of the other's actions.) Encourage your group to work with this question until people are able to see the necessity of each family member to give and receive forgiveness.

Question 6. Study the father's actions throughout the story from the perspective of how they might lead the sons to forgive each other. Focus especially on the closing conversation of verses 28-32.

Question 10. If it seems appropriate for your group, take a few moments at this point for silent or spoken prayers about the family members that they hope will forgive each other.

Question 12. If you want to tackle this subject with smaller questions (and if time permits), ask: What is hard (or impossible) about being a "friend" to your parents? What is hard (or impossible) about being a friend to your child? When did you first begin to think that you might be able to become a friend to one of your parents? to one of your children? What barriers have you seen to friendship between parents and children? How is friendship between a parent and an adult child different from friendship between peers?

Study 8. Loving Friends. 1 John 4:7-21.

Purpose: To imitate God's love in our relationship with him and with other people.

Question 1. Use this question to understand each other's history and to appreciate (and even laugh at) childlike ways of expressing friendship love.

Question 2. This question should help your group respond emotionally to John's concept of love while at the same time making a brief survey of the passage.

Question 3. Use this question to help your group examine the text in detail. People should point out information about God's love in almost every verse.

Question 4. This question builds on the previous one—as does the passage itself. Survey the text one more time as you look for links between God's love and our own.

Question 5. Move beyond the text at this point as you encourage your group to speak of practical ways this type of love might show itself in ordinary lives. Be aware that not all outcomes of this type of love will be mutually satisfying. God's love is sacrificial and so, sometimes, is our own.

Questions 7-8. These questions will require more personal answers than the previous ones—and in the difficult area of sacrifice. It is not easy to think of ourselves as being hard to love, or receivers of sacrificial love. Be prepared to offer an example of your own. Most of us will have to admit that we have at some time received sacrificial love from a parent, teacher, friend, spouse, or even God. After people in the group have been able to admit their own need for receiving sacrificial love, they will be a little less resentful of the loving sacrifices they must make in their own relationships.

Question 9. Contemporary society idolizes love. We can do almost anything "for love" and be met with indulgent smiles. This is not the teaching of the passage. Love is part of the core character of God. It describes who he is. But God is also faithful, wise, holy, even wrathful. And love (by itself) is not God. Your group should discuss its way to similar conclusions.

Question 10. The key here is, of course, the word *perfect*. Little in this fallen world is perfect—including love. So we often see fear and love mixed. Your group will think of examples of this mixture. Only God's love is perfect. As we attempt to model God's love (as this passage encourages us to do), we will begin to drive out the fear in our relationships.

Question 11. Encourage each person to respond in some way to this opportunity for personal reflection on the text.

Study 9. Jesus with Mary, Martha & Lazarus. John 11:1-44; 12:1-11.

Purpose: To use the loving friendship between Jesus and the Bethany family as a model for our own relationships.

Question 1. Give each person a chance to respond briefly.

Question 2. Use this question to survey the entire story. Your group should point out and discuss information in 11:2, 3, 5, 8, 16, 19, 20, 31, 33, 35-36, 40, and 12:2, 3, 7.

Question 3. Verse 4 mentions God's glory as a purpose. Christ's discussion with Martha in verse 25 explaining who he is and his power over death is another factor. The miracle of Lazarus's resurrection so soon before Christ's own death and the hope that this would later provide also comes into play. If your group has trouble with this question, try rephrasing to ask: How was Christ's delay an expression of love?

Question 7. Verse 2 tells us that Lazarus, who had spent four days in the grave, was eating with them—a visible witness of Christ's power over death. Verse 7 shows Jesus letting his friends know that he would die, which might make the event only a week away a little less shocking. Mary would remember this occasion as a loving moment when she was able to express her love (v. 3). She would feel accepted by Jesus because he accepted her gift (v. 7). During his upcoming isolation and torture, Jesus could remember the love that he received that night from all of his friends gathered there. They, in turn, would remember this warm and loving meal together.

Questions 9-10. Use these questions to once again think through the entire story, this time integrating it into personal faith and action. If your group has talked about many of these ideas in previous questions, give a brief summary and move into the final question.

Question 11. Your group should discuss the relationship between Jesus and Mary, Jesus and Martha, as well as the relationship between the two sisters.

Study 10. Friends Accountable to Friends. Galatians 6:1-10.
Purpose: To take responsibility for nurturing spiritual growth in each other.
Question 1. Try to get two responses from each person. You will use the answers to this question at the close of the session.

Question 2. Your group should define attitudes reflected by the words *gently* and *humbly* (v. 1). People should also notice the accurate self-evaluation described in verse 3, and that we are not to be competitive or put others down in verse 4. Verse 6 shows that we are to be generous, verses 7-8 that we must be aware of consequences, verse 9 that we should be persistent, and verse 10 that we are to be loyal.

Question 3. Your group should draw on information in verses 1, 2, 6 and 10.

Question 4. Warnings appear throughout this text. Your group should spot such words and phrases as "watch yourself," "tempted" (v. 1), "deceive himself" (v. 3), "test his own actions" (v. 4), "God cannot be mocked" (v. 7), "man reaps" (v. 7), "do not give up" (v. 9).

Question 9. One simple explanation is that we can expect to pay money ("share all good things") with people who give us spiritual instruction. Pastors, seminary teachers and missionaries would fall in this category. But the verse may also suggest that just as the instructors share knowledge and insight with us, we too can share what God has taught us. This reciprocal arrangement is illustrated in the relationship between Paul, Priscilla and Aquila, and Apollos.

Question 12. Encourage as many who are willing to respond. If your group wishes, make a list of intentions for the week and check up on each other's progress at the next meeting time.

Study 11. David & Nathan. 2 Samuel 11:1—12:25.

Purpose: To consider why (or whether) we should confront sin in friendships where we are accountable to each other.

General Note. As preparation to lead this session, read passages that deal with the past and future relationship between David and Nathan. These include: 2 Samuel 7:1-17; 1 Kings 1:1-14; 4:5; 1 Chronicles 11:38; 29:29-30; 2 Chronicles 29:25-26.

Question 2. Your group should point out events throughout the chapter. Allow time for comments about personal reactions to what David did. Potential "hot spots" appear in verses 1, 4, 6-8, 14-15, 25 and 27.

Question 3. Opinions may vary. Relevant information appears in verses 7-13. Some in the group may accept Uriah's noble statements in verse 11 at face value. Others may guess that Uriah was aware that something was not right about David's "friendly" gestures.

Question 4. Note David's calloused response in verse 25.

Question 7. If your group needs help with the symbolism here, ask that they figure out who in David's life symbolized the rich man, the poor man and the ewe lamb.

Question 9. Your group should find information in verses 13, 16-17, 20, 23, as well as the comfort he offered to Bathsheba in verse 24.

Question 13. Help your group to be as personal and specific as possible within the bounds of propriety. This closing scene shows us that not all accountability missions are ugly or confronting. Nathan brought good news from God, and we may also hear and receive commendation from our friends. God gave David a new start. God did not retract his previous promise to David that his descendants would rule Israel. God even passed his love for

David on to his new son. Some in your group may notice that if we confess our sins, God may also give us a fresh start—even if we can't fix what we've done wrong. (David could not bring Uriah back to life.) David suffered terrible consequences to his sin, and more consequences are yet to come. But God will not hold our shortcomings against us forever. He will keep on loving us. People in your group may express hope and comfort in similar situations.

Study 12. Forever Friends. 1 Thessalonians 4:13—5:11.

Purpose: To find comfort, warning and hope in God's offer of eternity together with him.

Question 2. Use this question to help your group study the entire passage—especially the vivid images it portrays.

Question 3. Your group should point out Christ's actions throughout this text. Note especially his death and resurrection and the term "and so" in verse 14. Paul's picture of our life after death is rooted in Christ's own victory over death.

Question 4. Survey the passage once again, looking for encouragement. What is encouraging will vary from person to person, but a composite will pick up most of what is in the passage.

Question 6. While the first passage you studied is full of hope and joy, this text mentions several warnings. Your group should mention such phrases as: "thief in the night" (5:2), "destruction" (5:3), "labor pains" (5:3), "not escape" (5:3), "darkness" (5:4), "wrath" (5:9) and others.

Question 7. Your group should study verses 4-9, exploring the variety of contrasts offered here.

Question 8. Verse 8 speaks of salvation as a "helmet," a form of protection. Your group should explain salvation as it is described in this text (vv. 9-10). They will find further explanation in 4:14-18. If some in your group are uncertain about whether they currently belong to the light or the darkness, explain as simply as you can the offer Christ makes. Invite others in your group to do the same.

Question 11. Invite everyone to pray brief prayers of a sentence or two as they look through the text. For example, you may begin by saying, "Thank you that you give me hope even though I still grieve the death of my mother." Help your group to be comfortable with silence between the prayers by suggesting that God hears our silent prayers as well as our spoken ones.

Question 12. Since this is the last session on friendship, use this session of prayer to thank God together for the friends he has given—including the friends within your own group. Again, suggest that people pray briefly are several times. End your time together by thanking God for the gift of friendship.

Carolyn Nystrom has written more than fifty children's books and Bible study guides, including three other LifeGuides, Old Testament Kings, 1 & 2 Peter and Jude *and* New Testament Characters, *and six Christian Character Bible Studies. Carolyn and her husband, Roger, are parents to four adult children and two sons-in-law. They enjoy an empty nest in St. Charles, Illinois.*

What Should We Study Next?

A good place to start your study of Scripture would be with a book study. Many groups begin with a Gospel such as *Mark* (22 studies by Jim Hoover) or *John* (26 studies by Douglas Connelly). These guides are divided into two parts so that if 22 or 26 weeks seems like too much to do at once, the group can feel free to do half and take a break with another topic. Later you might want to come back to it. You might prefer to try a shorter letter. *Philippians* (9 studies by Donald Baker), *Ephesians* (13 studies by Andrew T. and Phyllis J. Le Peau) and *1 & 2 Timothy and Titus* (12 studies by Pete Sommer) are good options. If you want to vary your reading with an Old Testament book, consider *Ecclesiastes* (12 studies by Bill and Teresa Syrios) for a challenging and exciting study.

There are a number of interesting topical LifeGuide studies as well. Here are some options for filling three or four quarters of a year:

Basic Discipleship
Christian Beliefs, 12 studies by Stephen D. Eyre
Christian Character, 12 studies by Andrea Sterk & Peter Scazzero
Christian Disciplines, 12 studies by Andrea Sterk & Peter Scazzero
Evangelism, 12 studies by Rebecca Pippert & Ruth Siemens

Building Community
Christian Community, 12 studies by Rob Suggs
Fruit of the Spirit, 9 studies by Hazel Offner
Spiritual Gifts, 12 studies by Charles & Anne Hummel

Character Studies
New Testament Characters, 12 studies by Carolyn Nystrom
Old Testament Characters, 12 studies by Peter Scazzero
Old Testament Kings, 12 studies by Carolyn Nystrom
Women of the Old Testament, 12 studies by Gladys Hunt

The Trinity
Meeting God, 12 studies by J. I. Packer
Meeting Jesus, 13 studies by Leighton Ford
Meeting the Spirit, 12 studies by Douglas Connelly